Living Inside the Meltdown

Ten people share their experiences of
Iceland's economic collapse

Alda Sigmundsdóttir

ENSKA TEXTASMIÐJAN

CONTENTS

Introduction   1

Drawing a Line in the Sand   8

The Hardest Part Was the Uncertainty   20

Force is Not a Viable Solution   28

People Are Returning to a Set of Real Values   41

The Crisis Has Made Icelanders Less Greedy   49

The Most Serious Thing to Happen in My Lifetime   63

It Turned out Better than We Dared to Hope   78

It Felt like We Were under Siege   86

Acknowledgements   95

About the Author   96

Introduction

In early 2010 I was commissioned to write an article about the effects of the Icelandic economic meltdown on normal Icelanders. It turned out to be a tricky assignment. The thing about the meltdown is that there was no one, across-the-board impact on "ordinary people." It affected each and every person differently, depending on their circumstances. Granted, there were some broad strokes, such as the loans indexed to foreign currencies that thousands of ordinary citizens had taken during the boom years. When the Icelandic króna plummeted in value, those loans doubled, tripled, or even quadrupled, and the payments became completely unmanageable for many individuals, who nevertheless struggled to meet their obligations. At the same time, thousands of people were suddenly out of work when certain sectors, like the building sector, collapsed. Those who did manage to keep their jobs almost inevitably had to accept pay cuts, as companies struggled to stay afloat.

Iceland's economic collapse probably attracted more media attention than any other event in the country's history, save for perhaps the volcanic eruption in Eyjafjallajökull in April 2010. Much of that attention focused on the big picture – the systemic failure, the culprits, the banks, the political crisis, the currency fiasco, the disputes over the Icesave banking accounts. But normal people suddenly thrust into the greatest man-made catastrophe Iceland has ever experienced have received very little press.

Fear and uncertainty permeated Icelandic society during those strange days in autumn 2008, extending to every nook and cranny of daily life. People worried whether or not they would have a job the next day, whether there would be food in the shops the following week, whether their children's playschools would stay open, whether Iceland would retain its sovereignty, and everything else in between. Nothing was certain, and from one day to the next everything that had seemed hands-down solid seemed fleeting and unpredictable.

No one was exempt. In a small nation such as Iceland it is impossible not to feel the impact of such a monumental event on your own skin. Each and every person had to completely re-assess his or her own worldview. We believed our society was virtually free of corruption and that an unwritten code of ethics was honoured by most people. Yet suddenly the veil was torn away and we saw a society rife with corruption, cronyism, incompetence and criminality – qualities most of us had associated with republics known for their banana production. Only this was *our* society.

It was traumatic, and like with any trauma, everyone has had to move at their own pace through various stages of shock, denial, anger and grief, towards some sort of acceptance. It has taken a long time, and as a nation, I don't think we are there yet. That said, parliament's fact-finding report into the bank collapse, published in April 2010, goes a long way in facilitating healing. The criminal investigation into the collapse, although it is expected to take years, will doubtless do the same.

Icelandic society is a curious society. There is an Icelandic saying: *Maður ber ekki tilfinningar sínar á torg*, which roughly translated means "You don't parade your feelings around in the town square." The Kitchenware Revolution, so called because thousands of Icelanders demonstrated outside their country's parliament buildings in January 2009 by loudly banging pots and pans, and which eventually brought about the collapse of the government, was remarkable because people were doing precisely that: parading their feelings around in the town square. I think one needs to understand Icelandic society to realise what a monumental event that was; how strong the feelings had to be in order to mobilise great numbers of people in that way. Iceland doesn't have a history of protests. Protesting is not considered couth in Icelandic society, and people who rock the boat have often been treated with suspicion and even derision. And upsetting the wrong people can be costly. That, too, is an Icelandic reality. Consequently there exists what the Icelanders call *þöggun* – silencing – at all levels of society, both overt and covert. Very often it takes the form of self-censorship so ingrained that it is no longer conscious, it just happens automatically.

And so, Icelanders don't open up easily to strangers. For that reason in particular I am very grateful to the ten individuals who agreed to share their stories with me. The subject of the economic meltdown is very sensitive for many people. Some struggle with shame, even though they have done nothing wrong and the circumstances in which they now find themselves are completely beyond their control. It's a strange kind of shame, an old kind of shame, something that lingers from an earlier time. Case in point: unemployment had not been a problem in Iceland for decades before the meltdown. There was always plenty of work to go around, and many folks worked two or three jobs.

When someone was unemployed, therefore, it was usually due to some kind of personal shortcoming – an addiction, perhaps, or a mental illness. Yet today, that feeling of shame about being unemployed still persists, even though circumstances have changed vastly. The national psyche has not kept up with the speedy developments of recent history.

The raw nerve that runs through the banking sector is a chapter unto itself. As most people know, Iceland's economic meltdown was largely caused by the overexpansion of the banking system and gross mismanagement of funds within the banks. The banks' owners and key executives were, and are, implicated in many serious matters, and some are under investigation for potentially criminal offences. Unsurprisingly, many regular bank employees feel betrayed and extremely angry. Most of the front-line people within the banks knew very little about what was going on in the upper echelons, and simply performed their jobs in good faith. In many cases they have been afraid to speak their minds because they fear it will affect their current or future career prospects. Sometimes they are working alongside people suspected of mismanagement, or worse. Moreover, they don't trust reporters, as many feel they have been double crossed or misrepresented by the media. It should come as no surprise, therefore, that finding people within the banks to interview – not only for this project, but also others – was incredibly difficult.

When I sat down to speak to the people quoted on these pages, I did so in an atmosphere of trust. These interviews should be read in that context. I was interested in sincerity, so I did not try to force anyone to go any further than they felt comfortable. I also tried to keep the tone as authentic as possible. In some cases I was asked to keep things off the record and I respected those wishes. Some interviewees also made it a condition that they would be allowed to read over the interviews before they were published, and that their superiors could also read them over. I was happy to oblige. I was, however, prepared to argue my point should a conflict arise as to whether something should be kept in or omitted, but it never came to that. Very few changes were made to the finished texts, and when there were, it was only to correct information or add something for the sake of clarity.

These interviews were done from January to March 2010 and are, in effect, a snapshot in time – a portrayal of the circumstances, feelings and opinions of the interviewees at that moment in history.

In several places in this book, reference is made to sums in Icelandic krónas. I know this may be confusing for foreign readers, but converting the amounts into other major currencies was not feasible in each instance. For anyone who wants a clearer picture, a currency converter is located at www.xe.com.

I very much enjoyed meeting the people who appear on these pages and I hope their sharing will give others some insight into the concerns, thoughts and feelings of Icelanders caught up in the most severe economic meltdown – relatively speaking – that the world has ever seen. I also hope it gives some insight into the fortitude and resilience of ordinary people coping with extraordinary circumstances.

Drawing a Line
in the Sand

Atli Steinn Guðmundsson *is 35 years old. He has a BA in Icelandic and at the time of writing is finishing his MA in journalism at the University of Iceland. He lives with his girlfriend Rósa Lind Björnsdóttir and her 13-year-old son Logi Snær. Their home is up for foreclosure due to default, and they own another property which they were not able to sell due to the collapse of the Icelandic real estate market. That property, too, is up for foreclosure. Atli and Rósa are among the many Icelanders who have decided to leave their home country and to start a new life elsewhere.*

In 2003, when I bought my first apartment, all was well with the Icelandic economy. The inflation rate was reasonable, and I hardly gave economics more than a passing thought. I had a BA in Icelandic and also a diploma in Applied Journalism. In autumn 2008 I decided to change jobs and go to work for 365 Media. When the collapse happened and my job ratio was cut, I decided to go back to school and do an MA in journalism.

In September 2008 I was working on the news desk at 365 Media and we knew that something big was about to go down. People looked at what was happening in the United States and saw that, here in Iceland, everything was going straight to hell, too. Still, I don't think anyone thought Iceland's three big commercial banks would collapse in the space of just one week. I remember that, in 2007, people were saying that Kaupthing and those banks just couldn't keep expanding. People were asking: What's going to happen if the banks go bust? But even when we saw Goldman Sachs and Lehman Bros collapse we thought this could hardly happen here. We thought we might be in for a pretty deep recession, but nobody had the imagination to think that, not only would the three major commercial banks go bankrupt, but the Central Bank, too.

When Prime Minister Geir Haarde addressed the nation on October 7 [2008], that was the point where I thought, holy shit, this is really serious. But, you know, I'm really quick to adapt to new situations and I'm naturally optimistic and to me it wasn't such a great a catastrophe as long as everyone was in the same boat. I thought: *I'm not responsible for this, I didn't do anything to cause this, there are thousands of people in the same boat*, and that made it easier to handle.

My girlfriend, Rósa Lind, and I started going out in February 2007. That fall we decided to move in together and to buy a house. By that time the Icelandic real estate market had already slowed down and more expensive homes like detached houses had practically stopped selling. Real estate agents were predicting that there would be hundreds or even thousands of properties on the market after the New Year that couldn't be sold. We decided to make an offer on a house. The set price was ISK 59 million [USD 459,000 in April 2010; currency converter found here], but as a result of the market slowdown we got it down to ISK 55.5 million.

Rósa and I both owned our own apartments at the time. Mine was mortgage-free. I had inherited money from my mother when she passed away in 2000 and invested in property. I owed nothing. It was a 100-square metre [1,076 square-foot] apartment that I bought for ISK 13.2 million in 2003. By autumn 2007, as a result of the real estate boom, it was valued at ISK 34.2 million.

Rósa decided to sell her apartment at the same time; however, right around then, the Icelandic real estate market froze. Had we tried to sell both apartments two months earlier, they probably would have sold instantly. Both were in locations that were among the most desirable in the Reykjavík area and the real estate agents assured us that there would be no problem, the properties would sell right away. We had no reason to doubt it. Rósa had put an apartment up for sale in that same area a few years earlier and it literally sold in two hours.

We finally managed to sell Rósa's apartment in September 2009, two years after it was first put up for sale. She had bought it in 2005 with a mortgage of ISK 12 million which was up to nearly 18 million by the time we sold it, due to the indexing of mortgages. So in the space of four years the mortgage had increased by ISK 6 million. And that mortgage was not even in a foreign currency, it was from the State Mortgage Fund. The person who bought the apartment just took over the mortgage and paid ISK 700,000 additionally. Any payments that Rósa had made on the principal during the time she owned it, plus her down payment – her total equity in the property – had disappeared. The real estate agent's commission, ISK 380,000 was higher than our profit from the sale.

As I said, we were counting on our apartments selling quickly, but when they didn't I took out an interim loan to make the down payment on the house. That was in March 2008. We thought we'd just be taking out a loan for a few days, just to tide us over. I went to a bank that was not my regular bank but which had a reputation for processing loans quickly. I mortgaged my apartment to take the loan. It was a foreign currency loan in Japanese Yen, which the bank claimed was the safest foreign currency to borrow in. We had not really looked into foreign currency loans before that, we just believed what the banks said – that they were the only loans that made sense because of the ridiculous indexing of the Icelandic loans [the principal on Icelandic loans and mortgages goes up in line with the consumer price index]. Besides, they claimed that the krona was very stable – after all, it had hardly fluctuated in six years. Inflation was already rising so we were relieved to get around the indexing. And foreign currency loans were so common – everyone was taking them.

I had no particular knowledge of economics and no idea how risky it was to take out such a loan. The banks were pushing them – they did nothing to warn people or reduce the public's expectations. This was at a time when most of us thought that if the banks said so, then it must be right, because the banks were so successful.

Then two weeks later, on March 17, 2008, the Icelandic krona suddenly plummeted in value and the loan started to go up. Over the next 16 months, that loan increased from ISK 17 million to ISK 43 million. From March 2008 and over the next six months, the loan went up by ISK 77,000 a day.

At that point I thought it had to be just a temporary fluctuation in the króna. It was bound to go back up again, the loan would go down, and we would sell the apartment.

Had our original plans worked out, based on the valuations of our apartments at the time they were put on the market, we would have owned our house today with just one mortgage of ISK 15 million. Of course we were also counting on both of us having jobs earning ISK 300,000-400,000 a month, which was a pretty average salary. If that had been the case, even if the mortgage had gone up to ISK 30 million, we could easily have made the payments.

As I said earlier, I was working for 365 Media when the collapse happened. My job ratio was 150 percent – I was a full-time journalist and reporter, and worked a 50 percent job as a proofreader on *Fréttablaðið* [newspaper]. In December 2008, two months after the collapse, my job ratio was cut to 37.5 percent. Rósa was working as an accountant for a legal firm, but was laid off in spring 2008. She got another job working for Samskip [shipping company], but two months later everything went bust and she was laid off again. She got a temporary job for three months, which was extended to six months, but ended, as planned, at the end of those six months. Rósa is currently unemployed, collecting unemployment benefits, whereas I'm living on student loans.

I never did manage to sell my apartment. It is rented out and there's no chance of selling because the bank won't allow it. It now has a mortgage on it amounting to ISK 40 million, but the apartment itself is valued at around ISK 25 million. A few months after the collapse, the Icelandic government requested that the banks offer their clients the option of freezing mortgage payments for a set period. I went to the bank to ask for that but they refused on the grounds that I was collecting rental income. I made a deal with them that I would just pay the interest on the loan and not pay anything on the principal. However, the interest payments on the loan went up to ISK 168,000 a month within a few months, while the rental income is only ISK 140,000 a month. When the interest on the loan became higher than rental income I decided to stop making the payments, which I had been making monthly from April 2008 to March 2009.

The mortgage on the house is a pension fund mortgage [in Iceland, pension funds issue loans and mortgages to their members]. The pension fund froze our mortgage payments for six months last year, as soon as we asked them to. But when that ran out, Rósa was unemployed and I had only a 37.5 percent job. Our mortgage payments on the house alone were over ISK 200,000 a month. It was obvious that we couldn't make those payments, not if we wanted to have money for food and to operate a car. We also had to pay for utilities and insurance on two properties, which amounted to around ISK 60,000 a month. So we haven't made a mortgage payment since January last year and foreclosure is imminent. We just got a foreclosure notification for our house last Thursday.

At this point, our debts are far greater than our assets. When our two properties go into foreclosure, the money generated from the foreclosure sale will go towards paying off our debts, but we will still owe the rest. Here in Iceland it's different from, say, the United States, where the lender simply seizes the property and you walk away from the debt. Here the lender seizes your property, sells it for whatever price he can get, and then goes after you for the rest of it for as long as he wants – until the day you die, if it suits him. In my case, my apartment might sell for about ISK 5 million, that is if the bank takes it over and no one makes a bid for it in the foreclosure sale, but it has a mortgage on it for about ISK 40 million. So I will still owe the bank ISK 35 million.

We owe about ISK 95 million right now. So we will lose everything except our furniture. I've come to accept that and I don't really care. I want to be able to keep my library of books – they don't confiscate things like that any more – but apart from that, we won't own anything else for them to take. They can send me collection notices for as long as they want, but I won't have anything to give them.

Since these are not debts owed to the state, like taxes, they can't go to my employer and claim my wages. Only taxation authorities can do that. When we move to Norway we'll just be on the rental market. We won't be able to own a car, but that's OK because the public transportation system in Norway is infinitely better than the one here and we won't need a car. Here it's virtually impossible not to have a car.

I have high hopes for Norway, it feels like starting over. But of course it's also a bitch. I'll be starting from zero in a new country. I had always planned to live in Iceland, all my education was geared towards living here, I have a BA in Icelandic and am finishing my MA in journalism. My education will have limited meaning in Norway or anywhere else, at least until I speak and write the indigenous language fluently. We had settled down and bought this house in a nice neighbourhood and of course it's annoying to have to abandon our plans – but it's really not much more than that. It's just annoying. In many ways we're doing great and we're feeling much better now that we've accepted our situation and decided to leave. And, I mean, you see people in the media who are in awful situations. Someone who owed a lot of money to [a company that issues loans for private and commercial vehicles] committed suicide recently. They confiscated his truck and he took his own life. And you hear interviews with people who have many children, or who are ill, or in whatever circumstances, and they can't go anywhere. But we are free to go. That's a luxury.

Some people say that those who stop making mortgage or loan payments are running from their obligations. They make them out to be criminals. The way I see it, the collateral for those loans is all there. The credit institutions get this house and they get my apartment – those mortgages were 50-70 percent of the value of the properties at the time they were taken. The fact that they went up by a total of ISK 40 million was completely beyond my control. They can't make me responsible for that. They're getting their collateral.

We made the decision to leave last summer. I had very high hopes for the Social Democratic Alliance [who won the national elections in April 2009]. I voted for them and I trusted [Prime Minister] Jóhanna implicitly when she talked about the "wall of shields" [a SDA election slogan; they promised to "raise a wall of shields" around Icelandic households]. I thought to myself, OK, now we have a left-wing government and they'll work this out, for sure. I was positive they would. I was jubilant when the left-wing parties won such a big majority in the elections. But they've totally let me down. Sure, they claim they're implementing measures to help the households, like lowering mortgage and loan payments by 17%. But I mean, who gives a shit about that when those payments are maybe ISK 400,000 a month and both breadwinners are unemployed? It changes absolutely nothing. The only thing they've done is change the law so that we can now take out our supplemental pension savings – take out our own money. Gee, thanks a lot!

Árni Páll [Árnason, Minister for Social Affairs] has absolutely no idea what ordinary people are going through. I mean, if I sat in a minister's office with a private chauffeur waiting outside, I'd probably think life was peachy, too. This guy was on the Kaupthing board when the banks were privatised, which marked the beginning of the entire meltdown, and he is now Minister for Social Affairs!

This whole mess started with the privatisation of the banks. Before that, the Icelandic banks were rock solid. I mean, Landsbanki was untouchable, it had been there for over a century, everyone had complete faith in it. And then, in 2002, a bunch of idiots bought it, came here with all this money they'd supposedly made from selling their brewery in Russia, which later turned out to be a total fabrication – or at least it was just half of what they claimed. It turned out they'd borrowed the money from another bank, Kaupthing, and Árni Páll was on the board of Kaupthing at that time. Now he's

Minister for Social Affairs. It's rotten to the core.

We have high hopes for Norway. We know people who have moved there and they have been incredibly well received. I know a guy our age who moved with his girlfriend and took his parents with him and they are all incredibly content. They can't imagine returning to Iceland. The Norwegians have shown the Icelanders a vast amount of support. They don't see us as losers over there, they're just very curious, and are wondering how a group of 30 people were able to bankrupt an entire country. I see this as a chance to start over. I just want to draw a big, fat line in the sand. It'll be just like I was when I was 18 and starting out, and that's fine with me. I'm totally excited about it. I think it's fantastic. For me, it is such a light at the end of the tunnel. I feel like I'm escaping, like I'm getting away. I don't see a future here. We've had three governments in a row that have done nothing for us. I don't see anything on the horizon here, at all.

The Hardest Part was the Uncertainty

Harpa Jörundardóttir *is 36. She lives in Akureyri, north Iceland, with her ten-year old son Gunnlaugur Gunnþórsson. She teaches English and Life Skills at the Akureyri Upper Secondary School. Harpa was studying in the United Kingdom when the Icelandic economy melted down. Without warning, all financial transactions out of Iceland were frozen, and Harpa and her son were left with virtually no money on which to live.*

I went to Nottingham in the UK to do my Master's in Professional Development in Special Needs in late August 2008. It was something I had been planning for a while. I had gone through a divorce a few months earlier and this was something I needed to do for myself. It was very important to me, both professionally and personally. I had been admitted to the programme about six months earlier, and at that time the exchange rate was ISK 128 to the pound Sterling. My tuition fees were GBP 10,200, which worked out to around ISK 1.5 million at the time. The academic year began at the end of September. By that time I'd been in the UK for just over a month, had enrolled my son in a British school and helped him get settled in.

I first heard that something serious might be happening with the Icelandic economy around the middle of September. My ex-husband called to ask what I had done with the money I'd received from the sale of our house. I told him it was in asset management at the bank. I intended to let the bank manage the funds while I was gone so I could at least maintain the principal and hopefully earn some good interest. The bank, Glitnir, invested it all in two funds – Fund 9 and Fund 1. They claimed Fund 9 was the safest, but in the end it was the one I got the least out of. I ended up only getting only 75-80% of my principal back. [Glitnir's Fund 9 is currently being investigated as a potentially criminal undertaking.]

My ex-husband told me he was sure the Icelandic economy was going straight to hell. He'd already transferred his money from Landsbanki to a local savings bank in his area. He's really good with money and has a knack for reading the markets. So somehow he was able to see the collapse coming and moved his money to a safe place. Personally I thought he was overreacting, that he was being too negative. Now obviously I wish I'd listened to him.

I had arranged it so that I could do my own money transfers online from my bank in Iceland to the UK. Then one day at the beginning of October 2008 I went to make a transfer and found that everything had been shut down. There was no way to transfer anything. I called my father in Iceland – he was not aware that the online bank transfers had been shut down, but he confirmed that the Icelandic economy was in deep trouble.

I'd heard some talk in the UK about a possible meltdown back home but not until that point did I understand how serious it was. There was absolutely no way for me to transfer money from Iceland to the UK. I called my bank, talked to some very nice people who were very supportive and completely understood my predicament, but said that unfortunately they could do nothing to help. Their hands were tied. The Central Bank had placed a strict ban on all currency transactions out of the country in an effort to protect the Icelandic króna. Without those restrictions, there were fears that it would collapse altogether.

They suggested that I use my VISA card. Then my father called and told me absolutely not to use it because VISA in Iceland was charging an insane rate of exchange. It was something like ISK 350 for the pound Sterling and ISK 280 for the Euro. The value of the króna had plummeted and the Icelandic government was trying to fix the exchange rate, but that's what the króna was worth on the European market. It was terrible for all those people who were on holiday and were using their VISA cards, expecting to pay the same rate of exchange as when they left, but then came home to find they'd been charged astronomical exchange rates, and they had no idea.

I had a little bit of money, but I had bills to pay: utilities, telephone and council tax. They came to around GBP 300 and I had just enough to cover that. I had no money left over, but my son had around 50 or 60 pounds that he'd collected in his piggybank. I told him we had no money and we would have to use the money in his piggy bank just to survive. That was pretty tough for a nine-year old. I said something had happened in the banking system back home and we couldn't get any money from there, so we'd have to scrimp and save until the situation was resolved.

For a period of about two weeks we had to live extremely frugally. We lived on packaged noodles and spaghetti with canned sauce and basically just as cheaply as we possibly could. We walked everywhere because it cost 4-5 pounds a day to take the bus and I needed that money to buy food. It felt awful. I had recently arrived in Nottingham, was still working to orient myself and didn't know anyone. I felt incredibly alone. I also felt trapped. I couldn't go home, had no money, and had a nine-year old child to support.

I had my bills on direct debit, so I called the electrical company and the phone company and explained the situation. They were amazingly understanding and helpful, told me I should just contact them when I got some money. They assured me it was no problem. I also got a lot of support from the university, even though they made it clear they couldn't wait too long for me to pay my tuition. As for my rent, I had paid six months in advance, so that was not a problem.

In many ways I was very lucky. The hardest part was the uncertainty that seemed never-ending. I didn't know whether I would get any money, and if so when, and at which exchange rate. The Icelandic Student Loan Fund (LÍN) had already granted me a loan equivalent to half my tuition that was sitting in my bank account back home. But when they paid it out to me, the exchange rate had had been around ISK 150 to the pound. When I finally managed to pay my tuition, the rate was up to ISK 280.

Fortunately, though, I was able to wait a bit and transfer the funds when the exchange rate was slightly better. I managed to do that only because my uncle, who lives in the United States, stepped in to help. He'd heard about what was going on in Iceland and called my parents to ask what my situation was in the UK, whether I needed any money.

He offered to lend me what I needed since he could easily transfer money from the US. So he sent me an express transfer which arrived just in time, because I was almost completely out of funds.

I was able to pay my tuition just a few days late. In the end, with everything factored in, my tuition fees wound up costing me over ISK 2 million, as opposed to the 1.5 million I had originally calculated. I'm still fairly angry about my loan situation. The money was paid into my account when the exchange rate was extremely low, and I had to exchange it later at a much higher rate. I think it's unfair that I should have to cover that loss. It made a substantial dent in my savings.

Nottingham lost a lot of money in the Icelandic bank collapse. The local authorities had invested a total of 42 million pounds in the Icelandic banks, and that money was completely lost. I thought I might experience some sort of hostility towards me just for being an Icelander, but that didn't happen. On the contrary, most people were incredibly kind and supportive. I was totally pasty and bleary-eyed from worry and lack of sleep and one of the other mothers in my son's school noticed. She'd heard about what was happening in Iceland, so she came over and asked how we were doing, if we were OK. Things like that meant a lot. The anger I experienced among the locals was directed at their own officials for having put all their eggs in the same

basket, not at me as an Icelander. I was just a normal person like them. If anything, people were worried about my son and me, even worried that we were under attack because of our nationality. I felt less support from people back home, especially LÍN, than the people in the UK. I thought there was very little understanding or empathy in Iceland about what we, the overseas students, were going through.

I think LÍN handled the situation badly. In my view they should have invited people in situations similar to mine to come in for an interview where they could go over each individual case and offer the relevant form of support. There aren't really that many of us, so it would have perfectly viable. Of course not everyone would have needed such measures, since some people were OK. But people like me who were taking a financial hit because of the exchange rate could have done with some support. For example, they could have sat down with me, gone over my situation, evaluated my loss and then arrived at a fair sum for compensation. Instead, I had to cover the entire loss myself. And it's not as though I was being careless with money. On the contrary.

Today I still have my money in the bank and am

renting an apartment for me and my son. I don't want to buy now – the housing market is too precarious and real estate prices are dropping.

I put my car up for sale before I left for the UK but fortunately no one wanted to buy it. It's a new Toyota Yaris that I bought in 2007 for around ISK 1.7 million. Had I wanted to buy that same model when I came back from the UK it would have cost me around ISK 4 million. I'm hugely relieved it didn't sell. I'm also hugely relieved I didn't buy it on a foreign-currency loan like so many people did in 2007. The car dealership was pushing the loan, strongly advising me to take it and claiming I'd make more money if I kept it in the bank and earned interest on it. But that sounded absurd to me. Why take a loan when I had the money and was able to buy it outright? So I listened to my inner voice and today I am incredibly thankful that I did.

Force is Not
a Viable Solution

Haraldur Sigurðsson *is 44 years old. He has been a member of the Reykjavík police force since 1986. Normally involved in investigations, Haraldur was called out with the rest of the Reykjavík force during the so-called Kitchenware Revolution – protests that shook Icelandic society from 20-23 January 2009 and ended with the collapse of the Icelandic government.*

Before the protests erupted in January 2009 the Icelandic police was very aware that anything could happen. The news desks had been monitoring the situation and we knew that the situation in Iceland was volatile.

Those three days of the main protests are a blur. I can't really remember what happened on which day.

I do remember that on the first day it was business as usual down at the station, everyone was working away on their own projects. Then at some point we were told to get ready and to go down to Austurvöllur [square, in front of the parliament building]. In situations like that, everyone is called out, even those of us who are investigators.

When that happens, you expect to be there a while – those are generally not brief assignments. You are expected to stand there until someone comes to replace you. That's something you learn right at the beginning of your career as a police officer. You are required to do your duty in all kinds of weather and under all kinds of circumstances. In this case our task was to protect Althingi – Iceland's parliament. Every police officer takes an oath that he or she will protect the constitution of the Republic of Iceland, and it is written in the constitution that Althingi is sacrosanct. Althingi must not be disrupted in its work. This oath, to protect the constitution and thereby Althingi, becomes second nature to us. It is in our blood and flows through our veins as police officers.

A fairly large number of us were dispatched down there, and there was utter chaos in the Althingi garden [behind the parliament building] when we arrived. It had filled up with people, both civilians and police, and there was major commotion. I will never forget the intensity. I realized just how new this was for us – not just us, the police, but also the protesters. I knew I was experiencing something very rare

for any Icelander to experience in the centre of Reykjavík. Vast pressure was building in one corner, where a new glass building meets the old Althingi building. It seemed like people were going to smash their way through the glass and into the building. There were a few police officers there, trying to prevent it, but they were completely outnumbered. It was so new; no police officer working today has been involved in the sort of civil unrest that we were witnessing. I was amazed to be witnessing this first-hand. I was also anxious. It seemed like anything could happen. We were equipped with pepper spray and clubs, some of us had helmets, and so on. The Riot Squad had been called out, so some of us were better equipped than others. The Riot Squad is a special task force within the Reykjavík police that is not deployed very often and its protective equipment is relatively new for the police force. This event caused me to think about the composition of Icelandic society in a completely different way. We have never had a military, and our society reflects this in so many ways. Look at the Icelandic police, for example, compared to police in just about any other European country. If something like this had happened in, say,

Spain or Germany or France, the police would have shown up with their clubs raised before they even started talking to anyone.

In Iceland we are taught that a police officer's club is either in its case or in his or her hand, and if it is in the hand, it is because the officer really intends to use it. I did not see a club in anyone's hand that day in the Althingi garden, and I believe that is because of what we have been taught – that force is only an option as a last resort.

All of this was going through my head as I stood there behind the parliament building. I also kept wondering: *Do these people really know what they want to do? All those news photographers in among the most radical protesters, do they know what they want to do?* None of them had any experience with this sort of unrest. They were just normal Icelanders with no experience of a rebellion of this magnitude.

That's when I started wondering if I was about to witness some kind of revolution. I was thinking ahead, about how things might possibly unfold and what my response should be. As police officers, that is what we are trained to do. To always think one step ahead. You want things to turn out well in the end. But in this situation, it was difficult to foresee what was going to happen because everything seemed so random and unfocused. I knew things could easily spin out of control.

At some point in the afternoon we started using

pepper spray to disperse the crowd. That only happens when someone in charge decides there is no other option. You have to have responses, and in this situation using pepper spray was deemed a necessary response. By that point the pressure to get into the Althingi building was so great that

the police officers were unable to withstand the push of the crowd much longer.

We were able to clear the garden soon afterward. We were getting notifications about protests starting up here and there and our challenge was to position officers in the right places. It was difficult because there were so few of us. The whole time I was very aware of that. People need to be able to take a break, even if just to use the rest room. And then you have to find someone to replace them.

We didn't really know what had set off the protests. While we were at the scene we heard snippets of things being said, like Althingi having an agenda for the day that in no way corresponded to the serious issues Icelandic society was facing. Things like discussing the sale of liquor in shops, and smoking areas in restaurants. I understand that was one of the major factors in setting off the demonstrations, but that was information that we the officers just heard in passing and weren't all that well aware of.

At some point someone had the brilliant idea to bring us earplugs. There was so much noise, people banging things, and it was really difficult to stand there. The earplugs made a huge difference. We formed a shield around Althingi. When we were able to take a break we went into the building where someone had ordered pizzas for us. People were laying down on the floor to rest. Everyone was completely exhausted.

In the midst of all the chaos I received a text message from my son, who is 12 years old. He was living in Norway at the time, and he had heard about what was going on in Iceland. The text read: *good night and may god's angel watch over you tonight during the protests. be careful dearest best daddy. please don't get hurt, be careful.* That meant a lot to me.

Most of us were there for a very long time. We had no other choice. I was there for 16 hours or more that first day. After being stationed near the Althingi building for a while I was called out to supervise a police van that was positioned at the site and that also went out on dispatches in the area when needed. When there were no calls for police assistance in the neighbourhood we remained near the Althingi building, but as soon as we got a dispatch, we got in the van and headed out to deal with that call. So we were taking posts at the Althingi building, then going on calls, then taking posts again. We were under enormous pressure the whole time.

One of our main tasks was to stop protesters from taking flammable materials from building sites to burn on the fires that had been lit in front of the Althingi building. They had already been taking pallets that they found in the area and putting them on the fire, and it was so big that the flames were the height of a two or three-storey building. We were trying to get to the sites before they did, to get rid of the flammable materials. That took up a great deal of time and energy. I was very lucky to have excellent officers with me – young people who are incredibly hard working and dedicated.

I also remember going to collect mattresses and blankets. We were preparing to set up camp in the Althingi building or somewhere nearby since we had no idea how long we would have to stay there. We also went to collect equipment like fire extinguishers, gas masks and so on. We were prepared for anything, using anything we could get our hands on. We didn't know where to store much of the equipment and as I was thinking about this I happened to see one of the ministers at the Dómkirkjan cathedral [located next to Althingi] and he gave me the key to the cathedral and permission to use it for storing equipment, if needed. The church was in no way involved in police operations, but everyone knew that the fire extinguishers would come in very useful if fire were to reach the cathedral. So the minister gave us permission to store fire extinguishers in the vestry. I thought it was quite appropriate because the vestry of the Dómkirkjan church was actually the first fire department in Reykjavík. It was where the first water wagon was kept.

I can't remember when I got home that first night, but it was probably sometime after midnight. I was completely worn out and frazzled. There was no way I was going to get to sleep right away. I started by saying my prayers, then I picked up some incredibly dull book and fell asleep.

I never looked on the protesters as antagonists. They were not my opponents. In my view they were people who had a perfect right to protest and I think most police officers felt the same way. On the other hand, we were there to do a job. Our main concern was that we were dealing with just a few individuals who were prepared to take things to the next level, who were prepared to destroy property or to inflict injury. They were out looking for trouble. Some of those people we'd had experience with before.

It is not easy to stand opposite an angry crowd and allow yourself to be pelted with eggs and *skyr* [an Icelandic dairy product] and having people spit on you. But I think most officers did not take it as a personal attack, because they don't base their identity on the notion of a 'militia' or something similar. There is not this major gap in Iceland between civilians and police. To most of us, the protesters were just people who felt let down. Their hopes and expectations had been shattered and they felt betrayed. It was clear that they felt Althingi had not fulfilled its responsibilities to them. They were angry and needed to vent.

As an individual and citizen, I also felt disappointed. I felt the people running the country had let me down. That was my personal opinion and probably also that of many of my colleagues who were protecting the building during those three days. But we were professionals and we were there to do our job. We left our own opinions behind. But that didn't mean I didn't have one.

At one point the violence had got out of hand and one officer had been seriously injured. Some people were publishing the names and addresses of police officers online and urging violence against them. Almost immediately there was this counter-movement, this surge of support for the police. It started on the Internet, and later, when the protests were coming to a head, a group of people broke off from the rest and positioned themselves between the demonstrators and the police, as a way of protecting the police from further violence. The next day, a few people brought flowers and gave to the officers on duty. That was a very unique experience and showed me more than anything else that the gap between us didn't really exist.

The situation was very alarming at the time, but I

think the protests ended in the best possible way. I truly believe that this was because they were permitted to run their course and were not beaten down right at the outset. But it was incredibly hard work and dangerous in many respects. Not only to protect the parliament building, but also the members of parliament. The Prime Minister, for example, came very close to sustaining injury [when protesters mobbed his car]. I have to say that the police did an excellent job, especially considering how under funded the police force is, and how few we are. In some ways I am surprised that those in power did not respond with a little more understanding for the predicament of the Icelandic police. Funding for the police has not kept up with developments in Icelandic society. The population of the capital has grown and violent crime has increased, and yet the police are suffering cutbacks. Had I been a politician under siege, with police officers protecting me with their own bodies, I might have thought twice about the sorts of conditions the police have to work under. I would have tried to use my influence to secure a bit more funding.

In many aspects of Icelandic society, there is a vast gap between those who make decisions at their desks and those who make them out in the field. In my view, decisions that are governed solely by bureaucracy are a major cause for concern.

Bureaucrats need to be in touch with the people, in my opinion, but sadly, this seems to have vanished. Politics seem increasingly driven by a mixture of greed, pompousness, arrogance, moral blindness, menace and lack of compassion. Who or what are the models for those attitudes? That is what I would like to know.

Iceland has no history of warfare, and more and more I am realizing how fortunate we are to have never had a military in this country. We have never had to train our young people for military service; we have never had to welcome survivors back home after a war. War has such a terrible impact on the social fabric of a country – people returning from war physically and emotionally battered and having to put their lives back together and to set about raising their children. We have been spared all that and we see those positive effects manifested everywhere. Iceland is still very safe. We can still confidently send our children unsupervised out to play. And there is a marked absence of walls and fences around people's properties. In just about any other capital city many buildings and private homes are protected by massive walls and fencing, which is virtually non-existent here. And all of this because it has never become ingrained into the mindset of the Icelandic people that the use of force is some kind of a viable solution. I think most people do not realize the immense value of this.

As I see it, this also applies on a wider scale throughout society, in traffic, child-rearing, sports, business ethics, and how solutions are arrived at in international disputes, to name just a few. Force as a means of oppression only leads to a chain reaction that cannot always be undone. Icelandic society needs to consider this aspect very carefully so it does not allow itself to become corrupted. It is very easy for a society to learn how to use force, but difficult or even impossible to teach those who have learned it from a very early age to stop using it.

We are fortunate to have had the US military stationed here because it prevented us from forming an army of our own. That could easily have happened in the last century. But instead of training an army we have been able to develop search and rescue teams on par with the best in the world. Some people say that you need to have an army to teach people discipline. But if people really want training or discipline, or if they want to wear a uniform, let them join the Salvation Army, or one of the rescue squads.

The traditional Icelandic term for police officer is *lögregluþjónn*, which literally means "law and order servant." Many members of the Icelandic police still approach their work in that way. The police officer is there to serve the public. To serve and protect. The role of servant is a noble role. And it is good when the police is able to approach its work in that way. I prefer not to use the term *lögreglumaður* ["policeman"], although it is much more common today. There are attempts everywhere to water down the "servant" term. I think this is unwise. I want to bring back the term *lögregluþjónn*.

On my desk I keep a pair of white gloves like the Icelandic police used to wear. I keep them there as a reminder. A police officer who approaches a scene wearing white gloves sends out a message that he is not about to engage in violence. To me, those white gloves perfectly symbolise what a police officer should be.

Looking back, I think it is very important that those protests were allowed to take place. Just about anywhere else they would have been beaten down by force. But here in Iceland the protesters were allowed to demonstrate for three full days and I think that says a lot about the position of the Icelandic police towards the protests. Essentially we were all in the same boat. We, the police officers, had taken an oath to protect Althingi and most of the demonstrators knew that was our duty. And we knew that they needed to demonstrate, to express their anger, and as long they wanted to do that, we had to keep standing there.

People Are Returning to a Set of Real Values

Gerður Gestsdóttir *and her husband* **Saul Gutierrez** *live in Reykjavík with their five-year old son Gestur. Saul, a house builder and architecture student, is from Nicaragua, where he and Gerður met. They moved to Iceland in 2002, then back to Nicaragua in 2007 when Gerður, an anthropologist, was recruited to work for the Icelandic International Development Agency in that country. They returned to Iceland in April 2009, some two months after the Icelandic government had collapsed in the wake of widespread civil unrest. On returning to Iceland they were both unemployed for several months before finding temporary work – Gerður with the government, supervising a programme aimed at helping adolescent children of immigrants find work, and Saul with the City of Reykjavík doing restoration work on a historic building.*

GERÐUR: We met in Nicaragua and moved to Iceland in 2002, just as the economic boom was starting. I began working for the Intercultural Centre in Reykjavík [a centre for immigrants, largely funded by the city] as a project manager. We moved back to Nicaragua at the beginning of 2007 because I was offered work there. So we were in Iceland when the bubble was inflating, but missed most of the insanity associated with the 2007-era. When we returned, we found a completely different society from the one we'd left in 2007.

My experience of the collapse was probably very different from most Icelanders because I experienced it remotely. I sat at my computer every day and read what was going on. I guess I started to realize something was wrong when the exchange rate started dropping, and then of course when all the trouble started with the banks.

Nicaragua is one of the poorest countries in the Americas, with around 70% of the population below the poverty line. I was working with the poorest people there, who didn't even have food to eat and weren't able to send their children to school. So to me, the crisis in Iceland was like what we in Iceland call a "luxury problem". I didn't really understand the deep emotional trauma the Icelandic nation as a whole was experiencing.

We returned to Iceland in April 2009, right

around Easter. The old government had collapsed a few weeks earlier and elections were just around the corner. There was this incredible jubilation in the air, this feeling of victory – or at least an interim victory. Our political leanings are Left-Green and just about everyone around us is the same. So there was this great sense of excitement. We felt like we could do anything – we'd win the elections and then we would have the first exclusively left-wing government in Iceland. To me, the Iceland I had come back to was a changed society, and there was enormous optimism.

For the first time in my life I experienced a feeling that people like us – socialist, left-green – were considered "normal" in Iceland. My political views have always been to the left and I have always felt like an outsider in Icelandic society. I felt that others viewed me as this annoying sort of person who was constantly nagging, who had these socialist views and who should just be ignored. But all of a sudden I was living in a society where my way of thinking was the norm. Not only that, it was totally acceptable. We had left Iceland when neo-liberalism was at its height and my way of thinking was considered profoundly uncool. But all of a sudden, everyone was like me.

So when "we" won the elections, the possibilities seemed endless. But then the shock came. The problems turned out to be huge and could not be solved overnight. That's when I started to realize how serious things were, and just how big those issues were. The government has been plugging away ever since, but things are moving incredibly slowly. We're looking at many, many years of rebuilding this society.

For us, the "unemployment metre" started ticking as soon as we moved back. There has traditionally never been a problem with finding work in Iceland, so this was very new. By summer 2009 we were starting to get worried that we might not find work. But we were amazingly fortunate in one respect: we sold everything we owned before leaving the country in 2007. That was the height of the boom so we got a good price for our property. So we owned nothing, and we owed nothing. Also, while in Nicaragua I received my salary in US dollars, so it was unaffected by the crash of the Icelandic króna. This meant we didn't have to worry about money for a while. Right now, our combined wages are about half of what they were before we left for Nicaragua in 2007. But still, we're doing fine. We've stopped travelling abroad, sure, but we're not lacking anything.

But even though we were OK financially, we lost big money in the collapse. We had put the full proceeds from the sale of our apartment into Fund 9 and it devalued by around 30%.

SAUL: That fund was a complete scam. It was being used to collect funds from the public, for the owners of the bank to use as their own private piggy bank. That money was stolen from us, and I find it hard to accept that the people who robbed us are still free, more than a year after the collapse. If we were in Nicaragua, those people would be in jail and all their assets would have been seized. I would like to know where all that money went. It doesn't just disappear.

When the banks ran into trouble, a woman we know was advised by her father-in-law, who works in a bank, to take all her money out of mutual funds and place it in a normal account. We sent an email to our bank advisor and asked if we should do the same with Fund 9. Her response was, no, Fund 9 has hit bottom and is beginning to go up again. She advised us to wait and see. A day or two later, the fund was frozen, and by the time it was opened again we'd lost several million krónur.

So much white-collar crime is rising to the surface now. In contrast to recessions in many other places, the kreppa is not just about economics or finance – it is also about all the corruption that is being exposed. The fact that the general public has to pay for the crimes of the bankers is horribly unjust.

In Nicaragua there is a permanent crisis. There is permanent poverty. But the difference is much more noticeable here in Iceland because there is this sharp drop in the living standard that happened with the collapse. In many ways the crisis here in Iceland is more psychological than anything else. It is about people having to adjust to a completely new lifestyle. Of course I know there are people who are losing their homes and so on, but I believe that for most people this is mostly about changing their lifestyle. And that can be very dramatic. The standard was very high and it is now being sharply lowered. And all of society has to adjust to that.

There was a similar economic crisis in Argentina a few years ago. When their crisis hit, people's salaries went down, and so did prices. Here in Iceland, salaries have gone down, but prices have all gone up because of the devaluation of the currency. That's hard.

GERÐUR: What always happens in situations like this is that those who were already near the bottom are pushed even further down. And we can't let that happen because those are the people who are most vulnerable.

I work with immigrants – people who came here to work during the boom years. Many of them do not speak Icelandic and they are having a hard time. The main problems they face are unemployment and not being able to get day-care for their children. These are people who are in much worse situations than Saul and I.

More than anything, I feel like the Icelandic nation has experienced a collective nervous breakdown. There is so much free-floating fear and anxiety; there is so much anger. Part of that is because people have the feeling that nothing is being done to apprehend those who are responsible. Justice is not being served. We know there is a committee working and some prosecutors have been appointed and so on, but we don't see any results. As soon as that happens I believe there will be an improvement in the psychological state of the nation.

The situation is very serious for those who took out loans in foreign currencies, to buy cars or even homes. I don't see that they are being helped out of their difficulties. It's like those issues are put on the back burner. It is an intolerable feeling to owe four times more than you own. It grinds you down. It is essential for the government to address issues like that.

For us, the hardest thing about living in Icelandic society after the meltdown is the nagging uncertainty. It's not hard to cope with adversity when you know what you're dealing with, but all this uncertainty is hard to take. For example, we both have temporary jobs and don't know what will happen when our contracts run out. And there is this vast ambiguity across Icelandic society, so many uncertainty factors and unresolved issues. What will happen with Icesave? How large are Iceland's debts? When will the oligarchs be brought to justice? And what will happen with public services? Already our son's pre-school has cut services; for example an art programme for five-year old children has been cut, and no replacement staff will be hired during summer closures, so there is a lot less flexibility. He starts primary school next year – what will be the situation then? What sort of an education will he get? What about other services, like public transport, access to health care, service for senior citizens?

So there is this vast uncertainty in all sectors of society, and a sense that things are moving in reverse. Iceland is not becoming a more developed nation, but the opposite. We really don't see the light at the end of the tunnel.

But of course, it is not all bad. The upside of the kreppa is that we finally have a left-wing government and a new awakening and awareness of what really matters in life. In the pre-kreppa years I often felt disgust at the rampant consumerism and greed. I felt completely out of place in that society. Now people seem to be returning to a set of real values. Things are moving more slowly and people have time to knit, spend time with their children and family. That is the positive aspect of this crisis, and it was about time.

The Crisis has Made Icelanders Less Greedy

Nuno Valentim *and* **Jorge da Silva Veiga** *are both from Portugal. Jorge came to Iceland in 2000 to work on the construction of the Smáralind shopping mall. Nuno and his wife came in 2007 at the suggestion of a friend. They were both working as manual labourers when the collapse happened – Nuno as a house painter, and Jorge as a construction worker.*

NUNO: I came to Iceland in April 2007. A friend of mine was living here and said Iceland was *great*. He told me we could have a very nice life here. In Portugal I had my own company and he asked me: What the hell are you doing putting lots of hours into a business that is almost bankrupt? I was earning the same amount as I could earn working at just a normal job in Iceland. So my wife and I decided to take a risk and try something new.

Of course, at that time the exchange rate was a little different from what it is now.

Our first jobs in Iceland were working in a fish processing factory in Hafnarfjörður. It took us one day to find those jobs. We began by staying with my friend, renting a room in his flat. We had brought some money with us, enough to get us started.

Soon afterwards we moved from my friend's place and rented our own small apartment. Our landlord owned a house painting company and he offered me work. I thought, sure, why not. So I learned how to paint walls and do all sorts of decorating. My wife saw an advertisement in the paper for a support worker at a pre-school in Garðabær. She applied and got the job.

My landlord, as it turned out, was a guy who liked to hire people to work black – illegally. I discovered when I went to the tax office that he had been deducting taxes from me but not paying them to the government. So I had no security. For example, I could not have collected unemployment if I had needed to, and if I had become sick I would have been in trouble. So there was a scene – I quit working for him and immediately moved out of the apartment. Thankfully we found another place to rent in Hafnarfjörður. It was very difficult to find something to rent at that time.

By September 2008, when the banks started

running into trouble, I had changed jobs and was working for a larger house painting company. I remember the collapse very well. The first bank, Glitnir, went down on a Monday. Everybody was listening to the radio. I went to the office to speak to my boss about what might happen. I took one look at his face and said: *This is not good.* And he answered: *No, it is not good.*

I knew the economy was not all right. The big fluctuation in the exchange rate was the first thing we noticed. I was sending money home to Portugal to pay off some debts so I was watching the exchange rate very carefully. But I was certainly not expecting a collapse. I mean, we've had these sorts of economic problems in Portugal for the last 50 years. We're used to the crisis thing. But I would never in a million years have thought all the banks would collapse.

So Glitnir went down, and then the next week, both Landsbanki and Kaupthing collapsed in the same week.

My wife and I had bought an apartment in summer 2008. When the collapse happened I was renovating it – painting the walls, putting in flooring, things like that. So my first thought when the collapse happened was, I've bought this apartment so we're stuck in Iceland. We couldn't just return the apartment. We had to stay and fight.

Around the middle of October 2008 we started

hearing rumours that the company I worked for was in trouble. It was without credit lines, had lost many contracts and would have to lay off a lot of people. I wasn't too worried, though, because my boss had told me that I would be kept on. I was a hard worker, I had my own car, put everything in the car and went out to jobs on my own. But then suddenly everyone was being laid off and my boss told me he was really sorry but he couldn't keep me on. This happened on the same day that we were moving into our new place. I had all my furniture in the back of the car and was transporting it to my new place when my boss called and told me I was fired. I went to pick up my termination letter with the furniture still in the back of my car. It was the hardest moment of my life.

Thankfully my wife still had her job at the pre-school even though they were cutting back on everything there. Some days she would come home crying and say they needed all these things for the kids and they had them in stock, but they weren't allowed to use them because they had to cut back. Things like napkins, or juice for the kids; fruit was rationed, each child could only have one piece, the bread was strictly controlled, and so on. It was very weird and she was really upset because she didn't understand what was happening. It was like we were in the middle of World War III. Really, that was the feeling all through autumn 2008. It was like being in World War III. Everyone running to the shops to buy food, the shelves were empty, the exchange rate was crazy, Geir Haarde was on TV trying to calm everyone down, the international media were going on about how Iceland was going straight to hell, people were losing their jobs, all our friends, *everybody*. Almost everybody around us lost their jobs, especially the people who were working in the construction industry.

I was not able to follow the Icelandic media very well at this time, so my information came from my friends, or the news in English, or the international media. We googled it to try to find out what was going on. I did not feel like I had an insider view, I was more like an outsider looking in, through the international media. I was only able to catch about 50% of what was going on at this time.

After I was fired I found another job as a house painter, but it was with a rather shady guy. He only wanted to pay us a very low salary, so I only stayed a few days. I was freaking out, I didn't know what to do.

At the beginning of February 2009 I decided to start my own business. I started importing boxes of goods: household products, kitchenware, mops and vegetable cutters, things like that. I bought one box with ISK 30,000, sold that box and bought two more, then bought four when I'd sold those, and so on. My plan was not to get rich; I just wanted to have work.

Today, I have achieved my goal. I have a full calendar of promotions, I sell many products, have a storage space where I keep them, and so on. But this did not happen overnight; things have sometimes been slow, then busy, with lots of ups and downs. But things are good now; I work hard to promote my products. I rent a small space in the malls where I do promotions. When I started my business I was on unemployment benefits but gradually as things have picked up I was able to reduce my benefits each month until I had full-time work from my business. Today I make a living from it.

It's not easy, especially the way the exchange rate is in Iceland today. There is also a lot of paperwork, duty and taxes and so on, which takes up a lot of my time every day. But I had a choice – I could either go back to painting, or washing dishes in a restaurant, or doing some other hard labour for low pay, or I could try to follow through on the idea I had. I thought to myself, if it works, it works – if it doesn't, then I can always go back to what I was doing before.

My wife is still working at the pre-school, and in the evenings she works from home. She comes home from work at 5 pm and then from 5 to 9 pm she works as a seamstress. We live behind a very well-known store in Hafnarfjörður, which we use as a sort of place marker – we can tell everyone, we live behind [the store], which makes it easy to find us.

I freaked out when I became unemployed. Right then I was determined that it would not get me down. I knew I had to do something, to work with the situation, so it would not get the best of me. One thing I think is very bad: there is no help in Iceland for people who want to start their own businesses. There are no tax concessions or anything to help relieve some of the pressure when you're starting out. In Portugal we get two years where we don't have to pay taxes on salaries. If you are unemployed and have a venture that you want to start, the government will offer many different forms of assistance to help you develop your idea. I was looking for support, something that would help me out, but I found nothing. All my life I have been a salesman, and I am very good at it. And today I can make a living from it. But it would have helped me a lot if I'd had some sort of support to make it easier. The only thing they offer you here is six months of unemployment benefits where your income is deducted from your total benefits each month.

JORGE: I came to Iceland in summer 2000 to work on building the Smáralind shopping mall. I was recruited by an Icelandic company. They were looking for workers outside of Iceland because there was a shortage of labour. There were people from Portugal, Sweden, Germany, Denmark, Poland ... people from many different countries. We were working very hard to finish Smáralind; it had to be finished in record time.

Most of the workers left Iceland when Smáralind was completed, but I decided to stay. I liked it here in Iceland, it was quiet and there was no stress. I worked for a number of construction companies over a period of several years, and finally I started work on the new Reykjavík University building.

Then, in September 2008, people started talking in the cafeteria about trouble with the banks. Some of the people I was working with owned shares in companies and those shares were going down in value really fast. Then the banks collapsed, one after the other. I was working with some people who had money in money market funds that was suddenly frozen. It was really bad.

I didn't really understand what was happening, even though our Icelandic colleagues gave me some information. They talked a lot about the collapse, about the names of the people involved, and how much money there was, and so on. But all that was a bit beyond me. I didn't know who those people were and the issues were really complicated. So I just had a general idea of what was happening and I knew it was serious.

I realized things were changing fast and nothing

would be like it was before. Before the collapse there was lots of work to go around, plenty of overtime, and work on the weekends for those who wanted it. But after the collapse our hours were gradually reduced. Overtime hours were cut, and then other hours, and finally there was hardly any full-time work. We also had to take a cut in pay. At the same time, everything was going up in price. Many of my foreign colleagues left Iceland but I decided to stay and see what was going to happen. Also because I had debts, so I couldn't just leave.

Today I am still working on the construction of Reykjavík University, but for a different company. I'm earning only about half of what I earned before. I'm making a living, but it is only enough for the basic necessities. I manage to pay my bills, my rent, but nothing more. I can't allow myself any extras – like going out for dinner, or on holidays, or even out for a few drinks. There just isn't any money left over. It's hard to see a future this way. Many of my Icelandic colleagues have found jobs in other countries, like Sweden or Norway, and I think I may look into that.

Immediately after the collapse, I noticed there was an increase in xenophobia and anti-foreigner sentiment. People kept asking me if I was going to leave, to go back home. My answer was that this was my home now. And in the cafeteria at work the Icelanders kept talking about the Polish people, saying that they were sending money back home. They were taking money out of the country, and they shouldn't be taking money out of Iceland. So I told them, don't worry, the Polish government has already sent ISK 200 million to help with the crisis, so you're getting it all back.

There seemed to be this attitude that people were just taking money out of Iceland. But the people who were sending money home were also producing something, and paying taxes in this country. And the crazy thing is that nobody says anything about the oligarchs. Look at all the money they took out of the country! But nobody says anything about them and they haven't even been charged for what they did. I think Iceland has to start charging the oligarchs and making them responsible for what they did, rather than making the foreigners into scapegoats.

NUNO: People also asked me if I was not going to go back to Portugal now that the collapse had happened. I told them: *Well, I thought of taking my apartment and putting it in a shipping container but I'm afraid the floor above it would fall down.*

Unfortunately, I think many companies in the building industry used the economic collapse as an excuse to get rid of people. They fired people, even good workers, and hired other people for lower pay. They used the collapse to send foreigners back home. In some cases people deserved it – those who slacked off, who called in sick on Mondays a lot, or didn't show up for work on Fridays. In cases like that it's understandable that they would have been fired. But there is no explanation for why really good workers were fired and others were hired in their place for less money. I think many companies were just using the opportunity to clean house. They wanted to get rid of the foreigners and give work to the Icelanders. They didn't care about the foreigners. Their attitude was that the foreigners would just go back home anyway, so it didn't matter.

I don't think the normal office worker in Iceland experienced this. The construction industry is really the underbelly of Icelandic society. There is so much shady and dubious business there. It's not like working in an office, where everyone is smiling and happy. If you work in the construction industry, you are "an immigrant." If you work in an office, you are "a foreigner."

We know a lot of people who talked about their employers putting pressure on them to quit. One of our friends worked in a welding company, and his employers were always talking about how terrible the crisis was and how our friend would have to leave. Finally he was laid off, but the day he came to pick up his termination notice, there were two new Icelandic guys starting. There were a lot of things like that.

JORGE: I feel there is a lot of pressure in Iceland for everyone to have the same opinion. We can really see it because we are outsiders. It often happened that I was sitting at a table with Icelanders where everyone had the same opinion. And someone else came out with a different opinion, they put pressure on him to think the same way as they did. I found it difficult because I normally have my own opinion, and that was frowned upon. In Portugal, everyone has their own opinion, and that's OK.

NUNO: Iceland is an open-minded country in so many ways. Icelanders are very open to certain things, like new gadgets, shopping centres, new technology and other things. But they still have this old-fashioned mentality. They think like a herd. I see this a lot when I am working in the malls, doing promotions of my products. For example, if a group of Icelanders come together to watch a demonstration of a product, and one lady says: *Hmm, I'm going to think about it*, then the rest will generally say that too, and they'll leave. But if someone says: *Oh wow, that's GREAT, I'll take it!* then the other people will buy it too, just because the first person decided to buy it. And that's without even seeing a demonstration of the product! In

Portugal, people want to see how the product works before buying it.

There is also a lot of pressure for everyone to be the same and to have expensive things. When I was working as a painter before the crash, one day my colleague, who was just a regular worker, came to work in a Land Cruiser. A Land Cruiser! He was just a regular worker! In my country people have a family car, but a regular person might drive a Peugeot, or a Citroen or something. Only rich people drive Land Cruisers, but here in Iceland it's like everyone has to have the biggest and best of everything, and everyone has to be the same. Right after the collapse, I noticed that people were ashamed when they were short of money. They would come to my demonstrations in the malls, and when they saw my products and liked them they'd say: Oh but I have to think about it, and they would leave. But now they say: I don't have the money right now, maybe next month after I get paid. They're not ashamed of that any more, it's OK for them to say that. I think that's good.

JORGE: I think the kreppa has made Icelanders think more about their spending. It has brought them down to earth. They realise they can't just get a loan from the bank for whatever they want to own. I think they are less greedy, they realise they don't always need to have more of everything. They have a better sense of balance between what they earn and what they can spend.

The Most Serious Thing to Happen in My Lifetime

Tryggvi Hannesson *is 75 years old. He has seen Iceland pass through many highs and lows, but feels that the current kreppa is the most serious thing to happen to Iceland in his lifetime. Tryggvi operated his own building supplies company in the 1960s and subsequently became an importer and wholesaler of building supplies. He has traditionally supported the Independence Party, but is disillusioned with how things have been handled over the last several years. He currently works for a chain of Reykjavík hotels, overseeing maintenance and running various errands.*

This is not the first kreppa to hit Iceland. This country has gone through all sorts of crises, both economic and social. For example, there was widespread unemployment in 1968 that led to a mass exodus from Iceland. People left for Sweden to work for Volvo or for the ship-building plant in Malmö. And in the 1970s we had hyperinflation. If you had 100 krónur you had to spend it real quick because the next day there was hardly anything of it left. The króna devalued steadily and our disposable income shrivelled up. At that time many people were building their own homes and one plank of wood might cost the equivalent of a week's salary. People were buying wooden crates used to transport Russian vehicles to Iceland, and used them for building. There is a whole neighbourhood in Reykjavík that was built from that kind of scarcity. As a nation it took us a long time to come out of that.

The Independence Party led by Davíð Oddsson came into power in the early '80s and that's when things started to improve. But no one talks about those hardships any more. The Icelanders are used to weathering both good times and bad, but during the good times, no one remembers the bad.

What we are experiencing now is not an economic recession. It's a recession caused by thieves. This recession is courtesy of those who robbed the banks from the inside. The situation is terrible and people are afraid to speak their minds about what's going on. I think they're afraid of the communists currently in power, because that's what this government is. A communist government. Jóhanna [Iceland's prime minister] is known for keeping her promises. But these days she seems to lie incessantly. When she first came to power, she said the main thing was to remove Davíð [Oddsson] from office. That was supposed to take three days. It took a month. Next it was the turn of the households; she was going to do something for the households. But she has yet to find those households. She can't seem to do anything for them. All the promises the current government makes are lies. Nothing ever gets done. The value of the króna is very low, we have currency restrictions and we're in a deep recession. And there's no saying when we'll climb out of it because they're all just playing in a sandbox and arguing about Icesave. They're supposedly negotiating with the British and Dutch governments but by the time they finally reach a settlement on something we'll probably owe twice what we do now, in interest alone.

I had my own auto repair shop from 1962-1964, then moved into importing and ran a building supplies company until 1985. I sold it and moved exclusively into imports and wholesale until 1999. I was satisfied with the way the country was run then, by the Independence and Progressive Parties. It was good, and everything ran smoothly, until they started with the heavy industry, all those power plants. There was a shortage of labour so people worked a lot and earned lots of money and could buy anything they wanted. They went on a spending spree, and travelled a lot, took holidays in the sun, that kind of thing. Then things started to turn bad and today people are lucky if they can afford to take the bus.

My son has just moved to the United States. He studied computer science in Sweden, came back and had trouble finding a job after the crisis hit. He tried for five months. His wife was working for an American genome company and her boss was being transferred to the US and asked if she'd like a job there. She earns a much higher salary over there, besides the fact that she's receiving wages in a proper currency. Not like here.

They bought an apartment up in Grafarholt [Reykjavík suburb] during the boom – paid ISK 24 million for it. My son owned an apartment previously so they paid out around ISK 12 million as a down payment. They were both working and both had a good income, so it was no problem. It was just the two of them with their son. They bought a car ... it was a walk in the park. Then he lost his job and suddenly they were a single-income family. They'd get up in the morning and check the rates on their mortgage, and every day they'd owe more than the day before. Their mortgage has now gone through the roof. I think it's up to ISK 40 million by now. And that's just a normal state mortgage, not even a mortgage tied to a foreign currency. That's the trouble today – you work and work to bring in money, but it makes no difference, you can never catch up. That is the reality in Iceland now.

Here's the thing: all these properties around here with mortgages on them – and I'm just talking state mortgages ... there is no use in trying to pay them off. You work and work and pay and pay, and the principal just keeps rising slowly and steadily, and you wind up never owning a thing. It's like paying rent. You never form any equity. But I don't believe the grass is greener elsewhere – it's a tough life for people who move abroad, too. It's not like every other place is overflowing with work, or that the cost of living is much lower than here. Just getting out of Iceland is not some foolproof solution. But granted, they don't have this problem with indexed mortgages in other countries.

The current interest rates are killing this society – the rates on the loans and the prime interest rate set by the Central Bank. Icelanders are slaves to the banks and the credit institutions. And when you work like a slave and you don't know anything else you become complacent – but deep down you know it's wrong. So you walk around with a long face, knowing that your money is being used to keep the banks above water. In my view, banks should be closed. No one should have to deal with a bank. They are hotbeds of corruption. Look at IceBank, which was run by Finnur Sveinbjörnsson, who today is running Arion Bank [formerly Kaupthing]. He drove it into the ground and then had ISK 700 million of his own debts written off. And what's he doing now? Doing deals with the Baugur empire behind the scenes? He refuses to say what he's doing. He won't say how big the debts are that he's planning to write off, but it's pretty obvious that over half of them will be written off. All of that will be done behind closed doors.

Just look at the banks' winding-up committees. All the thieves are sitting around the pot of gold that are the banks, wheeling and dealing in debts and writing off large portions of them. And the little people pay. They have lots of time on their hands, will work for low wages, and can always be sucked dry.

Steingrímur [Sigfússon, Minister of Finance] raised taxes but didn't realize that there were so many people unemployed that it wouldn't bring any more funds into the State Treasury. People who aren't earning a salary don't pay taxes. And manual workers, tradesmen and others will only work now if they're getting paid under the table. They don't even think about paying taxes. I know lots of tradesmen – I belong to a group that meets in the mornings for coffee. First they say, no no, we don't work under the table, but then after a while they admit that they do. There is plenty for them to do, so they just say: *I'll only do this job if you pay me under the table*. And most people say: *Sure, doesn't matter to me one way or the other*. It's the same with auto mechanics. Like when someone has caused an accident they'd rather have it fixed by a mechanic who is paid under the table than report it to the insurance company.

It's like we're returning to the East Bloc. We're seeing a shortage of goods in the shops. I go into [a building supplies shop] a lot, for example, and I'll see empty shelves, sometimes even along a whole wall. And I'll ask the clerks: *Will you have this in stock soon?* and they'll tell me: *Yes, it's bound to arrive soon*, but they sound pretty unconvinced. That shop is operated by the state now. It's been taken over by one of the banks. That bank keeps the people who bankrupted the company in the same positions and lets them run the company as before. The only difference is that those people don't care if the company makes money or not. They're getting paid well, so what do they care? They're not as invested in it, not like if they owned it themselves. It's a whole different way of thinking.

You hear about these cases now where the owners of the companies are getting them handed back after the banks have written off large chunks of their debts. Like the owners of Baugur Group getting Hagar back [powerful retailer with over 60% share of the Icelandic food sector]. That is insane. Under no circumstances should they be allowed to have it back. They [Jóhannes Jónsson and Jón Ásgeir Jóhannesson, the father and son behind Hagar] are the biggest thieves in the history of the Icelandic republic, in my opinion. When it comes to finance, they are the most dangerous men in all of Icelandic society, that's what I think. They have a 60% market share so they basically own the food market. They bought a share in Íslandsbanki [later Glitnir, then Íslandsbanki again] so they could have access to any amount of money they might need. All they had to do was to go in and take out the money. They could take billions of krónur out of the bank and didn't need any collateral! If you or I go to a bank and want a loan we need to mortgage our house, or get someone to co-sign for it. But for them, everything was wide open.

They now owe the Icelandic banks over ISK 100 billion. And they've managed to completely segregate wholesalers. They'll go to the wholesalers and say, I want this price, I want it to be *my* price, and I don't want you to sell the product to anyone else at this price. And the wholesalers are up against the wall, they can't say no because if they do then they threaten them with the loss of their business. Or they'll say: Isn't it easier just to come to me, instead of having to go to 20 different places? Tactics like that keep anyone else from entering the market. Just look at Jón Gerald [Sullenberger – arch nemesis of the Baugur camp who recently opened a discount supermarket in Iceland] – he's brought in this new store and has been trying to get himself established. He went to the wholesalers, and many of them refused to do business with him. Why? Because they were afraid it would upset Jóhannes and Jón Ásgeir. That's what you call domination and coercion.

Anyone who still shops at Bónus is supporting those thieves. I stopped shopping there a long time ago. My wife and I shop at Krónan now. People are so morally blind when it comes to this. All the things happening with Hagar, the debts being written off and the old owners being handed back the company, all this has been in the media a lot and the public is outraged, but they still go back to the same old place to shop. They're eating from the same old trough, rather than going elsewhere.

As for the other oligarchs ... I knew Björgólfur Guðmundsson [former majority owner and Chairman of the Board of Landsbanki] many years ago, when he was the Chairman of the Board of Hafskip. [Hafskip, a shipping company, went bankrupt in a major scandal in the 1980s in which four of its executives were indicted and Björgólfur Guðmundsson received a one-year sentence, suspended for two years.] He persuaded me to buy Hafskip shares. That man can't manage his own wallet, much less that the finances of anyone else. He started by bankrupting Hafskip. Then he bought a soft drink factory here in Iceland, disassembled it and took it to Russia to turn it into a brewery. They [Björgólfur and his son Björgólfur Thor] fell off the map for a few years, then returned with a freighter supposedly filled with gold and proceed to buy up all kinds of assets. But they never brought a single króna to Iceland. Why? Because they never owned that brewery in Russia. If they did, then where's the money? No one has ever seen it. Heineken bought that brewery from them, but no one has ever seen the money.

They supposedly returned to Iceland with coffers filled with gold, but the truth is they went from bank to bank to borrow the funds to buy Landsbanki. The government decided to privatise the bank and initially wanted distributed ownership, but all of a sudden there was this large core investor, which was Björgólfur & Co. and the plan about the distributed ownership went out the window. All of a sudden they were majority owners. We the public were told this was done because they were bringing so much money to the country, therefore they were allowed to buy the bank. It was a lie. They never had the money. Something like this wouldn't even happen in the worst banana republic. This country is filled with criminals who would have been assassinated if they'd lived in an African country. It's that simple. This would never have been tolerated. For people to walk around like counts and countesses – showing off, driving their cars worth many millions of krónur, flying around in private jets and all of that. The biggest surprise is that they were not attacked by the public a long time ago.

Yes, I am aware that the government handed them the bank on a silver platter when they privatised it. Of course they did. It's a mafia. It's impossible to flip over a stone in this society and *not* find that some MP or other is caught up in something shady. We had the revolution last year, people banging pots and pans, and what came of that? Nothing. The government continues to make promises, next month this is going to happen, the month after that something else – but nothing ever happens.

Personally I would like to get rid of all those idiots in parliament. I would like to see people appointed to work there, professionals with expertise in different areas, hired to do the job and supervised by the nation as a whole. The main institutions in this country are completely dysfunctional. The Financial Supervisory Authority is dysfunctional, the Ministry of Business Affairs is dysfunctional, the banks can do what they want, including playing their cards as they see fit. No one is regulating anything. Just look at the former rector of Reykjavík University [Svava Grönfeldt]. She sat on the board of Landsbanki, and just when things started to turn bad she sold all her shares and saved herself ISK 80 million. Who else had that kind of information? No one.

Or look at Illugi [Gunnarsson] in the Independence Party. He was the one who set up Glitnir's Fund 9. The operators of that fund convinced the wage slaves to put their money into Fund 9; they dug into the pockets of the little people. After that Illugi gets elected to parliament, and is he working to help the little people there? No.

I supported the Independence Party once and I still believe in its fundamental ideology, but I do not support its MPs today. Look at Þorgerður Katrín [Gunnarsdóttir] – how much has she stolen? Look at Illugi. Look at Tryggvi Þór Herbertsson and Bjarni Benediktsson. It's a cesspool. They were all part of the mafia. Anyone who wants to run for office is accepted only if they already fit with the existing mafia in the party and are prepared to play the game. You don't get anyone objective. It's impossible.

If you steal a lot, people look at you in awe. If you steal a little, you go to jail. If you steal a litre of milk from the store, the police turn up instantly and write up a report. If you steal a billion krónur, they don't even talk to you. Such is the Icelandic judicial system. It doesn't address a damn thing. They claim they're "investigating," but what good will it do to investigate for years and then have to sift through cases that are four to six years old? And say the person in question is convicted and has to pay such-and-such an amount, many millions of krónur, and they're already bankrupt? Where are you going to get the money?

Look at Eva Joly. She's recruited to come here, gets paid around ISK 1 million a month, they let her have a car and a house – and then you don't hear anything more. Sure, occasionally there may be something, but she's like a fortune teller with a crystal ball, just gazes into it and feeds you a lie. That's the only thing that comes from her. That's my opinion, at least. That's how I see it.

No way should Icelandic taxpayers pay for Icesave. It's not our debt. If I owe you several million krónur, the wage slaves should not have to pay for me. I should have to pay my own debt. And the people who wrote the directives that allowed the Icelandic banks to operate in those countries, they should take responsibility. The Icelandic nation is not responsible. Icesave was part of a private bank. It has not been definitively confirmed that there needs to be a sovereign guarantee on those accounts. The government stated publicly that they would, and then they stated publicly that they wouldn't. We should just say NO.

If the IMF decides to cut off our aid because we don't want to pay for the Icesave debt, a private debt, then let them. We're fine up here on the rock. We're on our way back to the mud huts anyway. We'll just eat our fish guts and our potatoes and whatever else. We'll be destitute whether we take on the Icesave debt or not. I mean, it's not like there will suddenly be money trees growing here if we agree to take on the debt. If we agree to pay for Icesave, there will still be a kreppa. The interest alone is huge. One hundred million krónur a day. If the government was receiving one hundred million krónur a day in taxes we'd be whistling Dixie. But instead we're heading straight to hell – and it's all because of the government. Not just this current government but also all the ones who've gone before. They all have their share of the responsibility.

The small-scale farmers will still be there. I am convinced that the Icelandic farming profession will survive this crisis better than any other. It is self-sufficient. Under no circumstances should we join the EU. That would be the icing on the cake. First Icesave, and then the EU. How many billions of krónur will it cost us to join? And what will we get in return? They'll take our fishing grounds, our waterfalls, our power plants, and we'll be sitting out in some hole in the countryside. It won't help us a damn bit.

We're fine with our own currency, provided that things are managed properly. We just need to get rid of those currency restrictions. We have enough exports to be a productive country that attracts foreign revenues. We have fish and aluminium, an abundance of power and so on. That's not the problem. The problem is how it's all being managed.

It is horrible to see what has happened to this society. This country has the potential to prosper if people just play their cards right. If it wasn't for those buffoons who laid everything to waste, we'd have a nice life today. This is the most serious thing that has happened to this country in my lifetime.

It Turned Out Better
Than We Dared to Hope

Sigríður Þorvarðardóttir *and her husband Paul Newton, who is British, are the proprietors of Pipar og salt, a popular cookshop in downtown Reykjavík. Pipar og Salt opened in 1987 and is known for having a British slant in its product range. It sells a host of quality items like kitchen accessories and linens, and non-perishable foods like preserves, mustards, teas and English biscuits. Like most business owners, Sigríður and Paul were hit hard by the sudden devaluation of the Icelandic króna.*

The meltdown came as a shock. I had no idea that anything serious was about to happen. When Glitnir collapsed I assumed it was just a one-off. I thought: *Surely everything will be OK*. It's just this one bank. But when the other two collapsed it became obvious that we were experiencing something out of the ordinary. It felt unreal. I kept thinking: *This can't be happening.* My thoughts were about things like whether I would be able to get my money out of the bank to pay for the goods I'd ordered; whether I'd be able to get them out of customs. I had a lot of fear and anxiety: *Will there be no money available? Will we have to close our shop? What will become of us?*

I remember the day Geir Haarde gave his God Bless Iceland speech [televised address in the first days of the meltdown] and a woman came in the shop and she was so afraid. I didn't even know he was going to make the speech, so I hadn't heard it. I remember my heart started racing and I just thought: *My God, what is happening?* It felt a bit like the terrorist attacks on New York, when everyone just stood there, so powerless, unable to comprehend the scope of it.

Of course it wasn't only about money being trapped inside the banks – there was also the devaluation of the currency. The value of the króna dropped by around 100% virtually overnight. All of a sudden our premise for running a shop seemed to have evaporated. Everything had doubled in price from one day to the next and we didn't see how we were going to keep the business open.

The currency restrictions were another big shock. I had always transferred payments to my suppliers through my online bank, but one day I went to make the transfer and it was blocked. I called the bank and was told that a ban had been imposed on money transfers out of the country, except with special permission. I would have to go down to the bank and fill out a set of forms explaining why I needed to transfer the funds and what they were for. It was literally like being set back in time about 30 years.

So I did as instructed, and my application was placed in a queue with a whole lot of other transfers. Transactions that had previously gone through instantly could now take up to three weeks to clear. And it stayed that way for about a year. It has only been a few months since those online transactions were reinstated. It feels like such a luxury now, being able to do them instantly, online.

So with the drastic devaluation of the króna, we were suddenly paying double for all our orders. We had a trade credit with our suppliers, meaning we already had the products in the shop and were selling them at one price, but had to pay double that amount when the payment came due. We kept hoping the rate of the króna would go up again, so we contacted our suppliers and asked if we could pay them when the exchange rate was a little more favourable. Some of them were incredibly kind and supportive and told us just to wait and see whether things improved. I'm an optimist at heart – I just kept thinking that things had to get better. But they didn't.

The meltdown occurred at the worst possible

time for us. For businesses like ours, the time around October is when we have our greatest expenditures because we're taking in the Christmas orders. We had been doing business with many of our suppliers for years and they had always provided us with a reasonable trade credit, perhaps a month or two. But all of a sudden they started demanding that we prepay our orders. Many of them were very apologetic – it had to do with the trade credit insurance they had, which lowers their risk in case of default from their customers. Those insurance companies suddenly pulled the plug on all insurance for Iceland. They no longer trusted Icelanders. That made things very difficult for us.

Most of our suppliers were very apologetic that they couldn't provide us with a longer trade credit, and of course we understood. But as I said before, some were incredibly kind and supportive and gave us a very good trade credit on their own, without the insurance company. This was especially true of our Scandinavian suppliers. They told us not to worry; we could just wait and see if the exchange rate improved. Some even gave us 4-5 months. We tried to pay everyone as soon as we possibly could, but unfortunately we didn't always have the resources to do so. Because we had to prepay some of our orders, we had less money to pay those suppliers who were offering us the most flexible trade credit. Which of course was terribly unfair. There were one or two suppliers who were very rigid and refused to show any flexibility, but in most cases we met with a great deal of understanding and empathy. Our suppliers were always asking how we were doing and how things were in Iceland. Amazingly, our turnover has increased dramatically since the meltdown. Contrary to what we believed at the time, our Christmas season in 2008 turned out to be excellent. In those two or three weeks after the banks went down, we hardly made a sale. Everything just shut down. For example, on the Tuesday when Geir made his God Bless Iceland speech we sold next to nothing. But then things started to improve and actually grew beyond our wildest expectations.

I believe there are a several reasons for this. First, we're small and have a wide product range, and many of our products are reasonably priced. There was a very noticeable shift in people's buying habits after the collapse. They still wanted to give gifts, but they chose smaller and less expensive things. For example, employers who might have given their workers a bottle of cognac for Christmas were now coming in and buying an English fruitcake or something like that. So we were getting new customers, and that has been the trend ever since.

Another factor is that Icelanders have started shopping at home to a far greater extent than before.

They are not travelling abroad as much, or if they are, they realize that it's actually cheaper to shop in Iceland now. Things have changed a lot in that respect. Third, there is the tourist trade. In 2009 we had about a 50% increase over the year before. Tourists, particularly Scandinavians, came and bought gifts to take home. Around 60-70% of all VISA transactions in June, July and August last year came from tourists.

Like everyone else, we have had to raise our prices over the past year and a half. But we have tried to be moderate and to take some of those cuts ourselves. We have lowered our mark-up by about 25%. If we had tried to keep up with our losses as a result of the devaluation we would have had to raise our prices by 100%, which was just not feasible.

It has taken us about a year to get back on track, to pay off all debts to our suppliers, lose the overdraft and other debts we accumulated as a result of the collapse. On the whole, we were very lucky. We're just a small company and we own our own premises so we didn't have any costly loans to pay off or anything like that. And we didn't have much money invested in funds or shares. We lost a little bit of money, but nothing to speak of. Also, our customer base is mostly middle-aged people, who were not the hardest hit by the kreppa. Some of them would even come into the shop and say: *This is not a kreppa. We have seen much worse than this.*

In order for business to flourish here in Iceland, though, we need to get rid of the króna. It is far too difficult to use a currency that fluctuates so much. It makes it very hard to make plans and projections for the future. And the króna is especially difficult now, of course. We've stopped importing from France and Italy, for example, because the króna has been so low against the euro. Our transport costs from those countries have also been very costly, much more than from the UK, for example.

Mind you, it factored highly in our decision that our suppliers in those countries were not willing to be flexible when it came to trade credit or other terms. They were very rigid. The Scandinavians and British were much more supportive. It was disappointing to us that even companies we'd been doing business with for 20 years were not willing to make any concessions. Not even to give us a five percent discount for prepaying the orders. I find that a bit harsh.

I'm definitely in favour of joining the European Union and adopting the euro. Apart from the stable currency, I simply think that Iceland should be a part of the international community. To me that just makes sense.

On the whole, I think this country has come out of the crisis better than we could have hoped. Things looked very bleak there for a while, but our worst fears did not come to pass. So at least that's something.

It Felt Like We Were under Siege

Kristín Jóna Kristjánsdóttir *works for Íslandssjóðir, a division of Íslandsbanki, as a portfolio manager. She joined Íslandsbanki in 2003, having previously worked at Landsbanki for four years. Her job involves determining investment strategies with her clients and managing their portfolios accordingly. Before the economic collapse this primarily meant investing in the stock market and in mutual funds, both domestically and abroad, but that has changed since the meltdown. Íslandsbanki changed its name to Glitnir in 2006, and back to Íslandsbanki in 2009. Kristín Jóna is 42 years old and has a husband and twin daughters, 12 years old.*

My job at Íslandssjóðir consists of managing the asset portfolios of my clients. I help them decide which bonds they should invest in, which today primarily means whether they should buy indexed or non-indexed government bonds. That's where the focus is right now since the market for corporate bonds has collapsed and the market for municipal bonds is very slow. As a result of the currency restrictions currently in place in Iceland we are no longer allowed to invest in foreign stocks and bonds, unless we are re-investing. In other words investors can re-invest the money they had abroad before the crisis, but can't make any new investments because we're not permitted to transfer money out of the country.

I joined the personal banking division of Íslandsbanki in 2003 as a portfolio relationship manager for individuals and smaller investors. That section was later split up and part of it was made into a private banking service for people who had more than ISK 100 million to invest. That's where I was working when the collapse happened. I stayed there until April last year, when I was offered the job I am in now.

I came to Íslandsbanki from Landsbanki, where I started working in 1999. Landsbanki changed a great deal when it was privatised in 2003 and I was very happy when I was offered a job at Íslandsbanki. I immediately felt at home there. It was – and still is – a very good place to work, despite everything that has happened in the last 18 months or so.

When I first started, the stock market was booming and people wanted to take risks. There was a sense of excitement in the air and of wanting to get in on the action. Not everyone felt that way, mind you – but many people did. Share prices sometimes rose by several percent a day. It was pretty exhilarating. We knew it would start to slide downwards again – that's the nature of the stock market. But none of us ever imagined that it would come to a total collapse. It certainly didn't occur to me, and I honestly don't believe it occurred to anyone else within the bank at that time.

When the Danske Bank report came out in 2006 [which expressed deep concerns about Iceland's economic standing] there was a slight downturn in the economy. That would have been a good opportunity for the banks and the regulators to implement some measures, to take those suggestions made in the report and act on them. Just to downsize a bit, issue fewer loans, not to buy so many foreign assets, or even to sell some assets. Of course we know now that the banks should never have been permitted to grow to the size they did. I don't know why our officials were so blind. It was like a collective denial.

There had been growing tension in the system for several months before the collapse and it kept increasing. The FX swap market dried up, for example. And just the atmosphere in general was tense. Clients were asking several weeks before the collapse whether Glitnir was going to go bankrupt. I told them no. I honestly didn't believe it was.

There was nothing in the bank's financial statements to suggest that it was going bankrupt. In October 2008 it was time for the bank to refinance a big loan and we were told that it had been able to do so successfully. But then Lehman Brothers collapsed and that set off a domino effect that the Icelandic system just couldn't cope with because it was highly vulnerable. The banks were far too big, and there was no capable lender of last resort. The majority of people working for the bank had no idea that it was about to collapse. When it did, it came as a huge shock and vast disappointment to those of us who over the years had worked hard to make the bank into a successful and thriving company.

I was in Sweden that fateful weekend before the collapse. My husband texted me to tell me that there were rumours that IceBank was about to collapse. It all seemed rather ominous. I came home on the Sunday, and on Monday morning when I was getting ready to go to work I switched on the news and heard that something serious had been going on with Glitnir over the weekend, that the lights had been on at the bank all night and things like that. It was the first I'd heard of it. The media were trying to interpret what it meant. It did not bode well.

When I came in to work at Kirkjusandur

[Glitnir's headquarters] I felt this immense tension in the air. It was indescribable. On that day there was this whole thing about how the state was planning to take over a 75% share in the bank. Of course it didn't do that in the end, possibly because everything was already collapsing and they saw they wouldn't be able to stop it. A few days later, of course, the government set emergency laws to safeguard deposits, and then the other two banks collapsed. It was an unbelievable week. It literally felt like a major catastrophe.

The very first effects of the meltdown were felt in my division, the asset management division, because that's where there was the greatest possibility of assets being lost. Those days were insane; it was like being constantly under siege. We were just trying to do what we could with the time that we had, furiously trying to sell stocks. The phone did not stop. I forgot my mobile phone at home one morning, and when I got it back two or three hours later there were around 16 missed calls, all from people who could not get through to me on the landline.

There was an enormous amount of pressure on us. I lost my appetite and couldn't sleep. It takes a lot for me to lose sleep, but during that week I hardly slept at all. But my mind was absolutely clear. It was like all the adrenaline went straight to my head and really focused my mind. I was completely immersed in what was happening. I lived and breathed it. I would go to work, come home and turn on the news, and just stay glued to the TV. I kept waiting for the government to do something – anything! I thought they *had* to have some sort of crisis plan – which turned out to be the emergency legislation they passed. Right up until

the day they did that, though, they kept telling people that everything was fine. Even the day before they set the emergency laws [Prime Minister] Geir Haarde appeared on TV and said that no special measures were needed! That really upset me. I knew otherwise. My reality was completely different from the one he was describing. I already knew the system was about to crash.

It really felt like Iceland had been attacked. That was the prevalent feeling everywhere and that was also the mood among our clients. Many people were extremely nervous and we tried to calm them down but they knew, like we did, that everything was collapsing. So we just did what the clients asked us to do. We didn't try to influence their decisions. We just tried to salvage what could be salvaged, to the best of our ability.

After the state took over the bank, around half the people in my department were let go. I remember someone saying that it was not easy to lose your job, but even harder to be one of the ones left behind, and that's exactly how it was. A really strange period followed. The atmosphere within the bank changed completely. For all intents and purposes it was a new bank, and there was a lot of uncertainty about the resolution of different issues for our clients. The working environment changed in an instant. One day it was all about the stock market, then the next it was all about debt equalization and debt resolution. I had no experience with that kind of thing and had to learn everything from scratch and learn it quickly. And obviously I wasn't the only one. I'm willing to bet there are a lot of Icelanders right now who are really skilled at dissolving banks!

I think the collapse was caused by a series of events, but part of the problem was that we, the public, were not sufficiently alert or critical. It's hard to be critical in this society. Everyone knows everyone else, and before the meltdown there were cliques everywhere, including all around the banks. The owners wielded a lot of influence. They never interfered in my work, but it certainly makes you wonder when you see the large claims Glitnir has issued in the bankrupt estates of some of the big companies that existed before the crash.

People lost faith in the system. No one trusted the banks anymore – not the public, not the clients and not the people working inside the banks. Most of us working in the banks were performing our work in good faith and had no idea what was going on behind the scenes. And then the system collapsed and all sorts of things rose to the surface and it was very shocking.

It's hard to describe exactly what happens inside of you. I didn't feel guilty, exactly, but I kept asking myself whether I perhaps should have seen it coming a lot sooner. I think most people have gone through that process, wondering whether or not they should have seen it. I think many of us

were left with this vague feeling of responsibility and a sense that we possibly could have done something differently.

At the end of the day, though, I feel secure in knowing that I always did what I thought was best for my clients. I can look at myself in the mirror and say with a clear conscience that I never went against my own better judgement. I really believe that is true of most of the people working within the banks. And that is so vitally important. It must be terrible to walk down the street and feel everyone's eyes on you and to be unable to hold your head high because you're ashamed of what you have done to your fellow citizens.

During the worst part of the crisis I made a conscious decision to start taking one day at a time. It was the only thing I could do. It was impossible to see any sort of future or predict how things were going to turn out. It's been like that pretty much ever since – this sense of not knowing what the future holds. There is still an enormous amount of uncertainty about everything. Mind you, today we had a strategic planning meeting where we tried to look ten years into the future. It felt really good to start thinking about the future again. Because it really has felt like everything has been on hold. We need to see something start to happen. We need to get out of the rut we are in and see a light at the end of the tunnel.

Acknowledgements

I have some people to thank. First, a big Thank You goes out to the people who shared their stories. In addition to having the courage to open up, they also took time out of their busy schedules to chat with me, and for that I am very grateful.

An extra big thanks goes out to my wonderful and talented husband Erlingur Páll Ingvarsson (EPI) who designed the cover of this book and fussed over it with me.

Major thanks also to Eliza Reid, who read over some chapters and offered helpful suggestions, and to Ásthildur Erlingsdóttir, Helena Einarsdóttir, Sigríður Ingibjörg Ingadóttir, Sigurður Jónsson, Toshiki Toma, Ásdís Sigmundsdóttir and Sigmundur Örn Arngrímsson, who all helped me find people to interview – or at least made a dedicated effort to do so.

About the Author

Alda Sigmundsdóttir is a writer, journalist, translator and blogger. She was born in Iceland, grew up in Canada, and has lived in the United Kingdom, Cyprus and Germany for longer and shorter periods of time. In addition to *Living Inside the Meltdown*, Alda has written one book of non-fiction: *The Little Book of the Icelanders*, a humorous take on the quirks and foibles of the Icelandic people. Her first work of fiction, *Unraveled – a Novel About a Meltdown*, was published in spring 2013 and has received excellent reviews. She has also published a book of translated Icelandic folk tales entitled *Icelandic Folk Legends – Tales of Apparitions, Outlaws and Things Unseen*. Alda is an avid blogger, and for six years wrote the popular blog "The Iceland Weather Report". She has also written extensively about Iceland for the international media. You can connect with Alda via her website aldasigmunds.com, catch up with her on The Iceland Weather Report Facebook page, or follow her on Twitter: @aldakalda.

Made in the USA
Middletown, DE
25 November 2019